Also by Betsy & Warren Talbot

Dream Save Do: An Action Plan for Dreamers

Strip Off Your Fear: Slip Into Something More Confident

In Confidence: Essays in Bold Living

Learn more about these books and creating the life you
want from the life you already have at

www.MarriedwithLuggage.com

Getting Rid of It

The Step-by-step Guide to
Eliminate the Clutter
in Your Life

By Betsy and Warren Talbot

Contents

Introduction

Step away from your dusty knick-knacks. Back off from the towering stack of boxes in your garage. Don't try to cram another piece of clothing into that overflowing closet.

We hate to break it to you, but you have too much stuff. Your home is overflowing with things you cannot even remember owning, and your junk drawer has spawned offspring. You need a month's notice for anyone to come visit you, and you can't remember the last time you were able to park your car in the garage. Your makeup drawer has mascara from 5 years ago and you own 17 pairs of black shoes, 11 of which look remarkably similar.

We haven't been spying on you, but we know exactly what you're doing. It is an epidemic, and not too many years ago we were in the exact same position.

How You Got into this Mess

You get conned into buying things for the life you want to have. Commercials and ads tell you that if you buy these clothes you'll look like the model wearing them, and if you buy this exercise equipment you'll have the perfect body, and if you have this kind of home / car / watch / purse / television / computer / jewelry you'll live happily ever after.

We're going to let you in on a little secret. Marketers get paid to sell you stuff, sometimes even stuff you actually need. But if you only buy what you need, advertisers won't make enough money to stay in business. You don't have to be convinced to buy food, shelter, clothing, and other necessities; but you do have to be sold on the "need" for a blanket with sleeves, a s'more maker, or a belt that magically works to give you six-pack abs while you sit on your bum and watch television.

In fact, think of all the money spent on treadmills every year when we could all just get outside and, you know, WALK. Advertisers depend on selling you more stuff to stay in business.

And when you aren't dealing with the advertisers preying on your wallet, you have friends and family and the threat of sentimentality to deal with. We think if we get rid of great-great grandpa's rocking chair, even if we never use it, we are disrespecting our family's heritage. We think we have to keep everything ever given to us by a lover, a friend, or a family member. We have been taught to show gratitude for gifts, even if we don't really want them anymore.

"What will Aunt Susie think if I don't wear that ugly Christmas sweater with reindeer on it that she gave me?"

Aunt Susie will get over it. And the bonus is that she'll probably stop buying you ugly sweaters because you don't appreciate her good taste anyway. That's a win no matter how you look at it.

Sentimentality and guilt account for a lot of our possessions, and we often harbor the mistaken belief that we have to keep these mementos to keep the memory or relationship alive. This is simply not true, and we're going to show you how to stop projecting your relationships and memories onto inanimate objects.

Finally, we're going to address the guilt - the guilt you have for spending so much money at IKEA or Bed Bath & Beyond or wherever your favorite Consumer Cult Outlet happens to be. You don't want to get rid of those things because you paid good money, dammit! (Or, conversely, you got such a screaming deal!)

This is a case of being penny-wise and pound-foolish. You will almost never make back what you spent on an item, especially when you consider the storage and maintenance costs for all these years. And it isn't a bargain if you don't actually need it anyway.

Get over it. Stop with the guilt. Move on.

How your clutter at home affects your life

There is a reason you feel claustrophobic in your own home. There is a reason you can't ever seem to get anything done. There is a reason you feel tired all the time. There is a reason you are not living the good life.

You are snuffing out your life with a mountain of stuff, and we're here to help you reclaim it. By getting rid of stuff you don't need you'll have more time to spend with your family and friends, to relax after a hard day at work, and to feel energized when you wake up in the morning.

You will be able to park your car in the garage to keep it cool in the summer and defrosted in the winter, starting your day off on a less stressful note. You will spend less time cleaning your house. You will stop making excuses to yourself and everyone else about why you can't do things.

You may feel overwhelmed right now at the idea of going through your stuff, thinking you just don't have the energy to start such a huge project or that you won't be able to part with your things. We're not your sister/mother/father/brother/best friends. We aren't going to throw any guilt your way, and we're certainly not going to judge you for the weird crap in your closets (when you hear what we found in an old dresser, you'll see there is *nothing* for you to be ashamed of!).

What we will do is show you there is a difference between accumulating stuff and creating a life.

You are going to feel 10 pounds lighter and hundreds or thousands of dollars richer very soon (you will be surprised which number is figurative and which is literal). You are going to see opportunities where right now you only see junk. You are going to have energy like you haven't had in years. In fact, you are going to be overwhelmed by what this very straightforward and simple act will do for every area of your life.

Are you ready for that?

Why You Should Listen to Us

Our names are Warren and Betsy Talbot, and in 2010 we sold everything we owned and left on an open-ended trip around the world. We've seen the wonders of Antarctica, explored the mountains of South America, cruised the Atlantic from south to north, dined on every good thing in Europe, and traveled by train across all of Asia.

It's a pretty good life for two 40-somethings who were members of the Cult of Consumption just a few short years ago. We had a big home in a great neighborhood. We filled it with nice furniture, artwork, clothes, cars, and even the damn treadmill we spoke about earlier (like you, we didn't actually use it for anything more than a clothes rack).

We woke up to the realization that we were profoundly unhappy with our lives and no amount of stuff was going to solve that. We set about making some changes in our lives right then, getting rid of the things that weren't core to the life we really wanted to live. Those things included material possessions – up to and including our house, a car, long commutes for our jobs, and living in an area that was not a good fit for us (childless-by-choice couples in their 30s should probably not choose to live in family-centric suburban neighborhoods).

We moved to a new city, changed our jobs, bought a small townhouse, and continued our plan of decluttering. We gradually stopped accumulating all the things that didn't fit into the life vision we had for ourselves. We learned to say no. We learned the huge difference between acquiring an experience versus a possession (one of those lasts forever and requires no upkeep or physical space). The less we had, the richer we felt.

Then in April of 2007 one of our close family members had a heart attack in his 30s. The next year a good friend suffered a brain aneurysm, also in her 30s. At the time we were both 37 and waking up to the stark reality that were weren't guaranteed a comfy retirement in good health with which to travel the world. At the same time the US economy was tanking, and we watched our retirement accounts bleed money every month.

Ready for a Change

It was both the most depressing and the most optimistic times of our lives. (*Wait a second; did they just say "optimistic?"*) Yes, you heard us right. Because we had already spent years downsizing and decluttering to only having the essentials to our dream life – things that were beautiful, useful, or truly meaningful – it took only a brief conversation to realize we could sell everything to travel around the world. And the very next day we started acting on that dream.

You may not want to sell everything you own to travel the world, but we didn't either a few years ago. What letting go of the junk in your life will do is open up possibilities you can't even comprehend right now, ***opportunities and experiences that just can't and won't happen while you are grounded by so much stuff***.

It will happen in small ways every single day as you get to spend more time in a comfortable space with your kids, your mate, or your friends. It will happen in large ways in the form of opportunities and ideas that you just don't have the mental energy to see right now, much less consider.

Find out much more about how we made our big dream of world travel happen – financially, mentally, and emotionally – in our step-by-step guide, Dream Save Do: An Action Plan for Dreamers (www.dreamsavedo.com.)

How to Use this Book

This book documents the system we used to get rid of all of our stuff in 25 months, how we made some serious cash doing it, and then set off to live the life of our dreams. Whether you want to streamline for a move, a big trip, a new relationship, or just to stop feeling so weighed down by all your possessions, this guide will show you how to get out from under all your stuff so you can start living the good life.

This book provides practical advice on getting rid of your stuff. However, we all know that a step-by-step guide isn't always enough. We also address the emotional and societal pressures of decluttering, and it will pay for you to analyze this as you strive to prevent a relapse in the future.

If you know why you tend to accumulate things, you'll see the warning signs earlier next time.

We'll be sharing a bit of our story as we go so you can see what it was like to get rid of those things at the time (two very different perspectives), as well as how it has impacted our present lives. To do that well, you first need to know a little bit about individually.

About Betsy

She is a recovering pack rat who was facing both the biggest challenge and greatest opportunity of her life when we started planning for this adventure in 2008. She likes to nest, things comfort her, and she doesn't easily let them go. She comes from a long line of pack rats – you could say it is even genetic! If you had told her at the start of our downsizing she would eventually be giving up everything she owned she would have probably thrown up on your shoes.

About Warren

He escaped Corporate America in 2010 after an 18-year career in the software industry. He has never met a piece of paper or item that he did not want to file or throw out. He absolutely loves to plan and could spend hours researching a new project or idea. He jumped headfirst into the process of getting rid of our stuff the day after we made the decision to travel. Needless to say this was not fully embraced by Betsy.

Getting Started

At the end of each chapter you'll find Weekend Challenges to help you reinforce your decluttering and downsizing efforts. Remember, the goal is to take decisive action on a regular basis, even if that action is 15 minutes a day. You'll be amazed at how much you can change your life with that kind of effort and impressed at what a focused push will accomplish.

Ready? Let's get started!

Chapter 1: Mental Prep

Before you start throwing things away willy-nilly, we should first explore a few schools of thought on the simplification process. It pays to know which system will work best for you both for this purge and for keeping yourself on track afterward.

Five Styles of Decluttering

None of these methods are "more right" than the others. In fact, the right one is the one that is easiest for you to do. The easier it is, the more likely you'll do it, and keep doing it.

We always advocate the easiest method because if it is too hard you simply won't do it. We aren't going to fight human nature; we're going to work with it to get the best results.

One thing in, one thing out

Are you happy with your space and number of possessions? Then this is the method for you. The vast majority of people are not here yet, but this is a good practice to put into play even now.

For example, say you recently bought 3 shirts to replace some old ones in your closet. Following this rule, you would immediately donate/recycle/trash 3 old shirts as soon as the new ones come into your house.

It may sound like a small thing, but this practice will keep you from accumulating more unnecessary stuff as you begin the work to declutter the rest of your house and set you up for good habits going forward. By adopting this process now you can stem the flow of things into your life.

Now that we carry everything we own in 2 backpacks this is the method we live by every day. While it was certainly not always this way, we love this approach whether you own 25 pounds (12kg) of possessions like we do or enough to fill a large home. Now we spent time thinking about every purchase and trying to determine what we need to throw away in order to make the acquisition. More times than not we end up passing on the new purchase and saving the money as well as the additional stuff.

Relieve yourself of a thing a day

Can you part with just one thing every day until you hit your simplification "sweet spot?" There are groups online documenting their decluttering efforts, and each post is usually a list of what was taken in as well as "relieved" that day. (It can make for some really funny reading, until you run across items you actually own.)

When you relieve yourself of just one thing a day you ha to keep in mind what you are taking in as well, so if you bring in a new book then 2 other things have to go to keep the number of possessions at a net -1 from the previous day. This method can be amped up based on your level of motivation on any given day.

The key to this method is to define a total number of possessions you want to get rid of or number days you want to do this. The nice thing is you can start off at 30 days and see big progress and get yourself used to the decluttering process.

Small is the new significant

Decluttering does not have to be a huge ordeal that takes entire weekends for a year.

The Japanese principle of Kaizen states that numerous small improvements done continuously are more effective than big improvements done sporadically.

Do you have 15 minutes a day to clean out a drawer, recycle old magazines, or combine your duplicate cleaning products? This is progress, and every day you can easily build on it by making another small continuous improvement. Remember, small is the new significant.

Getting started is often the hardest part of decluttering, and by promising yourself 15 minutes of daily effort, you'll often find yourself sticking with it for an hour or more. Once you get over the hump of starting, you'll be motivated to keep going.

One complete project at a time

It can be overwhelming to think of decluttering your entire home and office, especially if you are the only one who wants to do it. By breaking the job down into smaller complete projects, it will be easier to reach your goal.

If you have one day a month to devote to decluttering, think about a project you can actually finish. And by finish we mean completely decluttered, trash taken out, donations made, things sold or moved to the staging area (more on this later), and recyclables in bins.

If you leave any little piece of this undone, it will only add to your clutter and frustration. Better to completely declutter one closet than to attempt three (3) and have bags of clothes to donate in your garage for the next year.

Cash for clutter

You've probably seen those shows on TV: *Clean House, Clean Sweep* and the like. Part of the entire decluttering/organizing process in the show is a yard sale to raise money for redecorating. In each episode is seems the people are surprised at how much money can be made.

You can sell your items through a yard sale, online at Craigslist or eBay, or through consignment shops or specialty stores.

One key to this method is to have a "staging area" in your home. By removing the items from your daily life, you can continue your decluttering process until the item is sold.

Keep your staging area relatively small because the goal is to move it out fast, like inventory at a store. If you make it big, like the entire garage, you'll just end up with another permanent storage area.

One rule is to have a sell-by date - a yard sale on the calendar, a schedule for listing items online, or a date to deliver items to consignment and specialty shops. Otherwise, your staging area will turn into a huge clutter zone before you know it.

This is the area where Warren excels. He turned our house into a Craigslist shopping mall. Each week for 2 years he would put items on sale by taking pictures, posting them, and moving them down to our staging area (aka the Den). Every single time he did it we were one step closer to living our dream life, and the pileup of cash made it easier for Betsy to let go of her packrat tendencies.

What Style Works for You?

During our years of paring down we experimented with all of these methods and used each to different degrees. The one that proved the most fun (in Warren's words) was the cash for clutter system with Craigslist and our shared focus on small is the new significant.

The key is to dive in and start trying one out today. See how you feel after living with the new model for a couple weeks. Then you can try another until you find a fit with your goals and comfort level. In the end, focusing long-term on the one that fits you best will help you stay on track.

With a firm strategy in place, you will be able to easily dispose of your unwanted items and have a little extra cash in your pocket to celebrate your newfound simplicity.

Chapter 2: How to Sell Your Stuff

Before you start decluttering, you will need to decide what to do with all the amazing (but no longer amazing for you) items that will need a new home through the course of your decluttering extravaganza.

Some items will go in the trash and you'll wonder why you ever kept them (we had a set of broken coasters we moved with us between 3 states). Other items need recycling (such as old batteries). Still others can find a new life for a good cause at Goodwill, Salvation Army, or your local consignment store.

But what about the "good" stuff you think could garner a bit of cash if only you had a way to advertise? The extra TV (or 4 like we had), the treadmill you use for hanging laundry, or the collection of ceramic pandas stuffed in a closet could be worth something to a new owner and give you some extra spending money or savings towards your dream.

Does This Stuff Fit in Your Ideal Life?

When you sit down and think about living the good life, does all the stuff around you fit with your version of that idea? The more we worked toward living the good life, the more we'd look around and see the evidence of our past selves, the ones who spent all that money on stuff we didn't really need. We never knew we had a problem until we had a dream in mind and started to focus our minds toward making that dream a reality.

When we had a goal in mind, it became instantly clear what didn't fit. When you start thinking about how you want your life to look, it won't take a big effort to see what possessions are standing in the way of making it happen.

Craigslist (www.craigslist.org), Gumtree (www.gumtree.com), classified ads, and eBay (www.ebay.com) are probably based on the principle of reselling IKEA furniture and products. Instead of looking at your old IKEA purchases and feeling guilty, why not make a few bucks? It will also clear your space, which will help you better imagine your new lifestyle.

Believe us, someone wants your junk.

If you have smaller items to sell, or live in an area that doesn't have an active Craigslist audience, you can use eBay, yard sales or consignment shops. In the UK, Gumtree.com is another great alternative.

Again, you really won't believe what people will buy. Oh wait, of course you will. You bought it first! This is why Al Gore invented the Internet.

Craigslist (or Gumtree in UK)

This is by far our favorite; mainly because none of the items we sold ever fell into the unusual or highly valuable category. Over the years we've made over $8,000 dollars selling our stuff on Craigslist (see below for the story). The highest-priced item we sold was a dresser for $500 that wouldn't fit in our new townhouse. The least expensive thing we've sold is a random box of cords for $5. There is a market for just about anything.

Tips for selling on Craigslist or Gumtree

Write a compelling ad. Tell people more than just the description of the item. Get them to connect with you and want to buy it while supporting you at the same time. Every ad we put out we wrote about our trip and why we were selling things. The result was a great response to each item and a chance to engage with people. In addition, people were not as focused on trying to get a lower price when they knew the money was going to a "good cause."

Be honest in your ad description. Not everyone who stops by will actually buy, so don't waste anyone's time by claiming something is in excellent condition when it really isn't, or that it works when it doesn't. College students, the newly divorced, newlyweds – many of these people are looking for bargains and don't mind a little wear and tear, but they certainly don't want something that is not as advertised.

Always include a picture. The old saying, "a picture is worth a thousand words," could have been coined by someone trying to sell something on Craigslist. Many people search only for items with images so anything without one will reduce the number of people seeing your ads. Would you buy used items without a picture? Also, it is a great opportunity to show off your item without writing 1,000 words most people will never read. Take the time to get a good quality image with good lighting. The result will be in all those responses to come pick it up.

State "cash only" in the ad. Be very upfront about this and firm. You are selling to someone you don't know, and an honest face does not necessarily mean honesty where checks are concerned.

You get what you pay for. Ads are free and there is no online payment to guarantee the transaction until pickup. People are sometimes unreliable, and even when they show up they may decide the item is not for them. Keep in contact with at least two to three interested people so you don't have to repost the ad later.

Let your #2 and #3 buyers know you are holding the item for someone until X date and if they don't show or don't want it you will contact them back. You'll be surprised how often this comes into play.

Specify whether you will help them load or not. Someone who buys a large piece of furniture from you may want your help loading. If you can't do this or don't want to, make sure you state in the ad that you cannot load so they know to bring help. You don't want to lose a sale over the issue of loading, especially since these tend to be the higher-priced items.

Are you willing to negotiate on site? Once someone is there to pick up, they will occasionally try for a last-minute bargain. This isn't necessarily a bad thing; you just need to be prepared. Our favorite tactic was to have a "staging area" of all our for-sale items and offer something smaller and harder to sell in addition to the main item while staying firm on the price. For instance, when selling a chair offer a small area rug or throw pillows to go with it. The buyer gets more than she asked for, plus you get rid of hard-to-sell items.

Craigslist and Gumtree are free, and you can easily set up an account and start selling within minutes.

How we made $8,000 with Craigslist

Our love affair with Craigslist began back in Boston in 2004 when we first started our downsizing efforts. We were living in a 3,000 square foot home with all the furnishings and stuff that we thought we needed to fill it all up. When we made the decision to move to Seattle we knew we needed to get rid of a LOT of our stuff. Seriously, why did 2 people need 4 TVs?

We had never used Craigslist before to sell anything and were a bit tentative. However, it seemed like the right approach since it was local and we could probably sell things within a day or so of listing them – and, more importantly, get them picked up by the buyer.

We started by putting a few pieces of furniture up – a bed, couch, treadmill, and a TV. Warren wrote up the ads, took a few pictures, and posted them on a Friday evening.

By the end of the weekend we had sold everything and had a couple hundred dollars to show for the effort. Over the next 2 months we sold about half of our possessions since we knew we'd be living in much smaller accommodations in Seattle. Everything was done via Craigslist.

When we arrived in Seattle we found there were a few pieces that simply did not fit in our new 1,000 sq ft townhome. Immediately we logged into Craigslist and started the process again. By this time Warren's ad writing skills had reached poetic proportions and the dresser we both loved sold within a day for $500 (still our most lucrative single sale).

Once we made the decision to travel and started selling everything we owned we knew that selling it online was going to be the best approach. Warren put together a system. Once we agreed (or Warren convinced Betsy) we no longer needed something the process began in earnest:

- Take photos of the item

- Move it down to the staging area (our den)

- Write out a compelling ad for the item. Warren focused the ad on why people would want it as well as our story and why we were selling it

- Respond to every person who contacted us. This was a great help for those times when the original buyer did not show up

- Once cash was received put it immediately into our trip fund

Looking back we have made in excess of $8,000 through the 3 phases of decluttering (in Boston, when we arrived in Seattle with still too much stuff, and when we decided to take the trip around the world). It was done over time, but these are the specific steps we used to pull in this extra cash, which we are using today in part to fund our new lives.

eBay

eBay is a great resource if you have quirky items, collectibles, or are interested in expanding the market for your things. Perhaps your collection of vintage lunchboxes is no longer how you want to portray yourself to everyone who enters your home. Or you have a beautiful vase that no longer fits your decor. Anything a collector would look for is perfect for eBay.

eBay is an auction, and your potential buyers have time to bid on your item until closing (and with luck creating a bidding war). You set the minimum bid so that you will never lose money. The flip side is that if your minimum bid is too high your item may not sell. Regardless, you control the process so if you believe your precious collection of 3-headed ceramic turtles is worth $1,000 then you can set the price. We're sure someone in the world may share your unique passion, though we'd suggest a bit more perspective when you put items up for auction.

You will need to set up a PayPal account and register as a seller on eBay to be able to post your items. While neither of these is hard to do, it will take a bit of time so be sure to allocate an hour to learn about the process and all the sign up. Alternatively, if you want to bypass that and have someone do it for you, you can always look for an eBay reseller to do it for you for a percentage of the profits (just Google "ebay reseller" + your city).

The same rules for Craigslist apply to eBay:

- **Be clear and honest** in your product descriptions and photos.

- **Let potential buyers know about delivery.** (UPS, postal service, pick-up only, etc.)

- **Specify payment options**. Some eBay sellers take checks, but we don't recommend it.

- **Buy it Now**. eBay works on a bidding system, but you can also specify a "buy it now" price. This price should be between your minimum bid and what you expect it to sell for. The "buy it now" price is for the convenience of both parties.

Setting Up Your Staging Area

Now that you have decided on method (or methods) you will use to part with your more valuable possessions it is time to take the big step of identifying things to start with.

Setting up a "staging area" is one of the most powerful steps you will take in your decluttering project. This should be an area that you can store things that are in transition to a new home and life. Ideally this would be a room near your front door for 3 reasons:

1. This will encourage you everyday to get your items listed and sold. Seeing the pile dwindle is a wonderful motivator to sell more, and if you don't get it done quickly you'll eventually trip over it.

2. It will be a place you can invite Craigslist buyers into to see your items before they purchase. This will keep you from having to bring people through your home each time you sell something.

3. It also works as what the marketers call an "upsell" option. When someone comes to buy something like a camera from you, they may spot an end table or umbrella stand they also want. You just never know what people will like. If they know this is your staging area of things for sale, they will often make you an offer, especially if you make them a bargain. People cannot resist a bargain. You get the bonus of selling it without even having to advertise it.

An Alternative to Selling Online

Not everyone is excited at the prospect of having strangers come to their home from an ad on the Internet. We get that. Another great option for getting rid of your stuff is to invite your friends and acquaintances to shop through your house. When they know you are on a decluttering spree, they are more inclined to come by and pick through your goodies than when you only have a few things for sale.

We did this near the end of our decluttering process and when our house was in the process of being sold. We were able to keep our necessities until moving day, when our friends showed up to pick up their goodies. It helped us know exactly what we had left to sell without the inconvenience of sleeping on the floor or eating with our hands.

If you aren't getting rid of everything you own, you can adapt this plan to your situation by specifying a particular room, a type of sale (artwork, kitchen supplies, sports equipment, etc.), or even by place a small sticker on everything that is for sale (or everything not for sale depending on which one is easier).

How to have an indoor sale

- Buy some small yard sale stickers or post-it notes in bright colors. Pick one to be your "keep" color and tag every big item you plan on keeping as well as drawers/cabinets full of items you are keeping.

- Invite a few friends to go shopping at your house. We had 5 to start because it made it easier in our small space. It may make it more appealing to your friends if you include a list of some of the top items for sale.

- Give each friend a specific color of sticker and a pen and allow her to roam the house picking items she likes by putting a sticker on it. You can have your friends write an offer price on the sticker or do all their shopping, tell you what they want, and let you come up with a bulk price for everything.

- You negotiate payment and pickup terms with your friends that allow you to use your stuff until the very last moment, which makes the transition much easier. If you aren't moving, they can take the items that very day.

- Your friends really do want to help you and can be great sales people. Our friend Karen, for instance, called us soon after she left because she thought of a buyer for our bed. Sight unseen because of her recommendation and description, someone bought our bed and picked it up on moving day.

- This indoor sale is perfect if you are too lazy to have a yard sale, have a hard time parting with your stuff, or have a lot of good friends. You don't have to price anything, set anything up, or advertise other than an email or Facebook post to your friends.

- You do, however, have to have a reasonably clean and organized space. Remember that people will be looking around your house and opening doors and cabinets unless you tell them not to.

- Offer some light food and drink for your shoppers so they'll stay longer and either buy more things or help you sell items to your other friends. Warren had a lively negotiation with one friend over some furniture, and I think it was more fun for most people to watch that interaction than it was to leave with their new things.

Chapter 3: Sentimental Value is Assigned by You

If you don't already honor it, it isn't special.

Okay, this is where it gets tough. We know you have the best intentions and a real desire to get started on a decluttering project. You wake up on a Saturday morning and wander into your office/closet/basement with big plans to see the floor before the end of the weekend.

You open the first box and crash hard into Memory Lane. Suddenly you get sidetracked with flashbacks and feelings of "I can't get rid of this." Before you know it Sunday night has arrived, you haven't showered or changed all weekend, and you are sitting in the same spot with a bottle of wine and a pile of your stuff strewn about. You might even be sniffling into a tissue.

Getting Sidetracked

This happens to all of us. We find a treasured item in the bottom of a drawer or long-neglected and dusty in a closet. "Oh look, a statue of the Eiffel Tower from our honeymoon!"

Let's be honest here. *If an item is truly valuable to you, you will not lose track of it or forget about its existence.* You will use it often or look at it regularly. At the very least you will know it is being saved and is securely packed away with a specific intention in mind.

These "discoveries" can derail your project faster than lightning. You sit on the floor with the contents of a few drawers around you and simply run out of steam before you even get started. Instead you just dump it all back in the drawers and pick back up life exactly where you left it – stuff and all.

We're not saying that every item of sentimental value should be thrown away - far from it. We're saying that you assign sentimental value in both word and deed, and if you have chosen not to honor and take care of a particular item in the past, what makes you think you will do it in the future?

These are the kinds of decisions that make decluttering such a tough process for most of us. We believe that by getting rid of an item that once meant something we are somehow getting rid of the memory. Not true.

It bears repeating - you assign sentimental value - and when something is no longer sentimental it may just mean you've already processed those feelings and carry them with you.

A Lesson from Accidental Loss

How do you handle losing something of sentimental value? This is a question we contemplated often as we downsized our life in preparation for this adventure. Betsy's story below captures what many of you might feel about a particular object.

"I bought a ring in 2001 from a street vendor in New York. It was October, everyone was still in shock from the terrorist attacks, and I had just completed a year of personal upheaval and a cross-country move. So many things were going through my head at that time, and the previous year had been both more fantastic and more heartbreaking than I could have ever imagined.

The ring wasn't expensive, but I loved it and wore it often. It reminded me of being scared to death but doing big things anyway.

One evening in the midst of our preparation for this trip I lost the ring while out to dinner with a friend. I didn't even notice it was gone until the end of the evening, and by then it was too late to retrace my steps.

At first I was really upset because of all the things that ring represented and how much courage it gave me when I was scared or unsure of myself.

And then I had a moment of clarity.

The ring didn't give me courage. The ring symbolized all those experiences and emotions, but it didn't contain them. Sure, it is nice to have a visual reminder, but without one does it mean those experiences don't exist? Or that I will forget all the lessons I learned?

Have I been giving the power of those emotions and experiences away to material things?"

Defining Value

Value = the experience of travel. False value = receipts and tickets from travel. (Why have we been keeping these?)

Value = a love of reading/learning. False value = books we will never re-read. (Why haven't we shared them with others?)

Value = Clothes that fit our lifestyle and us. False value = high heels and suits from our old corporate lives. (Will we ever forget what big business taught us?)

Think about those love notes from your first boyfriend/girlfriend in high school. At the time, they were probably the most important things you owned. And now? It is likely a sweet memory that exists even without the actual notes. The same is true for most of our "sentimental" items, and having too many reminders of things that don't need reminding keeps us from valuing our current sentimental favorites.

You don't have to agree with us on this, and we suspect a few of you will cling to your "discoveries" and vow to keep them exactly where they are stored today. That's okay. We're just asking you to be open to the idea that the item is no longer needed to feel the emotion or to access the memory.

Tips for Letting Go

Take a picture and put the item in a box to donate/recycle/sell. Look at the picture every day for a month and decide at the end of the month if you really still need the item. Is the picture enough to trigger the fond memory?

Share the item with a friend or family member who could still appreciate it. Betsy had a set of china from her great-grandmother that was used only once in 20 years. Her mom has it now and is able to use it more often, and Betsy gets the pleasure of seeing it on visits and knowing that it is being taken care of. She no longer needs the china set to remember her great-grandmother. (Betsy: "my favorite memory is actually her saying "good gravy!" when she was surprised, and I can think about that anytime I want, clutter-free").

Write about the item in a journal. Talk about why it means so much to you and why you can't let go even though you know you should. This is a great exercise in self-discovery and may help you to work through why you need to hold on to things.

Weekend Challenge

Congratulations, you now have the groundwork for your decluttering project. At this point you have learned:

- How clutter impacts us

- 5 strategies for decluttering

- How to sell unwanted items

- How we put sentimental value on items

Now it is time to put all this knowledge into action:

Decide which decluttering strategy(ies) you will apply

Determine how you will sell/recycle/trash your unwanted items and make a plan (set up a PayPal account, set aside a staging area in your home, have boxes available for sorting, etc.)

Think about your definition of sentimental value and how you want to honor special items. If a "discovery" doesn't meet existing criteria, it will be easier to let it go.

Let's get started!

Chapter 4: Kitchen

The kitchen is the heart of most homes. It is where we prepare our meals, eat, recap our days with each other, and sometimes do our homework or pay the bills. It is probably the busiest room in your home, and therefore the one that gets cluttered the fastest.

When you spend the time to make this space roomy and usable, you make the large amount of time you spend here more pleasant. You won't be too overwhelmed to think about cooking a healthy stir-fry because the wok is hidden in the back of the pantry under all those other pans. You won't have to dig through the freezer to identify the mystery meat for the evening meal. You won't be scared to open the refrigerator because of that funky smell you know you'll eventually have to investigate.

You're going to love your kitchen again, and that will make your life better every single day.

Tables and Countertops

Flat surfaces are dangerous for most of us. We see a counter and find something to put on it. Schoolwork, craft projects, folded laundry - just about everything but a regular meal ends up on the dining room table.

Think about how you use the flat surfaces in your kitchen.

- Are the counters cluttered with kitchen items that are rarely used?

- Do you have stacks of mail, kids' schoolwork, or electronics on the bar?

- Could you have dinner at your dining room table tonight without a major cleanup?

Clear surfaces allow us room to work, enjoy good meals with family and friends, and clean up easily. Even more importantly, clean surfaces relieve tension in our lives that comes from having to look at this clutter each and every day.

Your first decluttering goal is to simply pick up the paper and excess stuff on your counters and find a home for it.

If you pay your bills in the kitchen or the kids do their homework at the dining room table, make sure you have a system for it so it gets cleaned off after each session.

Is it convenient for you to recycle? If not, you'll be cluttered again in no time.

Do you keep a blender/toaster/French press on your counter even though you rarely use it? Find a place in your pantry or cabinet to store it.

Make your kitchen counter truly a food prep area and not a storage facility. Think about where these things are going and how you can keep them stored properly going forward.

Our goal for decluttering the counters centers on mail, electronics, and kitchen appliances.

Here is how we used to treat our flat surfaces: We would stack mail on the bar and charge cell phones, cameras, and the Kindle there. Betsy's purse was typically on the barstool below. What does all this mean? Our bar was unusable for its intended purpose. We're not sure the barstools had been used more than 2 times since we bought them since there was always something stacked on them.

Because we lived in a townhouse before leaving, space was at a premium. There was really no need to keep appliances on the counter if we were not going to use them every day.

When we finally cleaned our counters off, we were able to converse with friends who stopped by for coffee or a glass of wine, we could easily see out from the kitchen into the living and dining area, and that simple action made our home more open and enjoyable every day.

What about you? How can you declutter your countertops today?

Defining Enough

When it comes to decluttering your kitchen, it is easy to focus on cleaning and stacking things neatly. It is a quick fix and something that does not require much physical or emotional effort. It can also be just the beginning of a larger project.

But before you start stacking and scrubbing, first make sure you need all that stuff. Organized does not equal decluttered.

Do you really need 24 plastic drinking cups (especially the super-size kind)? When you have so many of one item it makes it easy to let the dishwasher stay full while you continue to use all the excess items. Over time, there is a stack of dirty cups next to the sink and a full dishwasher that has yet to be run or unloaded.

By counting on so much excess, you actually make a bigger mess. And you take up valuable storage space.

Here are some items that are often overstocked in a kitchen:

- Plastic cups

- Plastic tubs and lids (aka Tupperware or takeout containers)

- Cooking utensils

The decluttering goal today is to take a quick count of your items. Once you find excesses (which depends on the size of your family and lifestyle), start trimming.

Some things to consider:

- Two people in your house and 16 dinner plates? Can you even fit 16 people in your home for dinner? If so, store at least half the plates in a china cabinet. If not, get rid of half.

- Five spatulas that look exactly the same? If you run your dishwasher regularly, you shouldn't need more than 2 so donate the rest.

- Dozens of plastic grocery sacks under your sink? Recycle them at your local grocery store and leave only what you will really use (cat litter, doggie bags, etc.). A canvas bag works better for transporting items from the grocery store, will save you space, and be easier on the environment. Just keep them in your car or by your door and you can quickly grab them while walking out the door.

   If you are thinking, "But I might need it later..." – keep reading.

The Box Test

One trick to deciding what to keep and what to throw away is the box test. Put all your excess items in a box (or 2 or 10 – however many you need) and store them. Use only what you have left in your kitchen and see how well it works for you. You can always add the items back if you really need them, and if 30 days (or whatever time period you set) goes by and you don't use something, add these items to your staging area and get rid of them.

The second tip works the opposite way and is great for decluttering your cooking utensils. Take all of your utensils (yes, ALL) and put them in a big box. Each time you need to use something remove it from the box and put it in back in your drawer.

At the end of a month, what is left in the box is what you donate/sell. The assumption here is that if you don't need it in 30 days (or whatever similar timeframe you choose) you can probably live without it forever.

When we went through this process we were shocked at how many extra utensils were left in the box at the end of the month. It was a true wake up call and a big step in our decluttering of the kitchen.

What can you do today to declutter your dishes and utensils?

The Pantry

Your Pantry: The place where cans of cream of mushroom soup and boxes of brown rice go to die a slow, lonely death.

Even if you are an organized person, you may have way more food than you actually need, which means it will likely expire before you get to it.

Size doesn't matter

Large pantry, open shelving, small cabinet - it doesn't matter what you have. We all overstock with items we will never eat and fail to remove them when they expire. Instead of solving the problem, we complain that our pantries aren't big enough or we go out and buy organizers of every shape and design to clean up the space.

After having 10 different kitchens as adults, we've come to a shocking conclusion about pantries: Size really doesn't matter. It is all about technique - shopping and storage technique, that is.

Are you overstocked?

Take a good look at your closet/ shelf/ pantry/ cabinet. Follow the steps below to bring some order and remove any food that is no longer good to eat.

Throw away any expired food and recycle the containers (this includes spices). We actually moved a large container of oatmeal from Massachusetts to Seattle and it was still unopened - and it expired 4 years earlier.

Will you actually eat what's left? For any food that you know you won't eat, put it in a box to take to the local homeless shelter. We stopped drinking Slim-Fast for breakfast when Betsy gave up milk, and yet we still had 3 containers of it 6 months later. Go figure.

Can you combine any products to save space and keep items fresh? For instance, you can put all your dry spaghetti noodles into a plastic container - same with beans, rice, and other pasta. We also did this with nuts, dried fruits, and cereals.

Now that you are down to the basics, think about sorting by how you use food instead of by height or category. If you rarely use canned soup, it should be on the top shelf even though it is small. This will make it very easy for you to see when you need to replenish what you use most.

Get a small notepad and attach adhesive to the back and stick it to the pantry door. Write down exactly what you need to buy when you first notice you need it. This will help you stay on track with your budget because you won't buy 2 cans of tomatoes from memory and come home to find out you actually needed 2 cans of tomato paste.

Even though our small pantry cabinet was a mess to start, it actually only took us just 20 minutes to declutter and sort. Besides the 3 cans of Slim-Fast that we no longer used, we found 1 big container of oatmeal, 1 bottle of lemon-pepper spice, 2 boxes of Jell-O and 3 cans of soup that had expired. That's a lot of junk in one small cabinet.

Some shopping tips to keep your pantry from bulging:

Buy loose spices and store in your own containers. They will be fresher and cheaper than the bottles and take up less room because you only buy what you need.

If you are organized enough, you can plan your meals in advance and shop weekly/monthly. This was hard for us to get into a rhythm with, but we know several people who did this successfully. One of our friends even taught classes in the Seattle area on "investment cooking" - aka "cook for a day and eat for a week/month." Check your community college or personal chef association to find a similar class in your area.

The other extreme is to shop daily or every other day so that you always have just a little bit of fresh food on hand. This is easier and more pleasant to do when you can walk to your grocery store and fairly common in larger cities. Now that we've been traveling for so long, this has become our daily habit in cities all over the world.

Have you tried online shopping? One way to keep from going overboard is to use a grocery delivery service like Amazon Fresh, Safeway or Peapod for your bulk shopping. Over the years we used all these services with success. You may also have smaller delivery services available in just your area, especially when it comes to local fruit and vegetable delivery. Google "CSA in (your city name)" to find one near you.

The Refrigerator and Freezer

Do you have a system for your refrigerator or do you just put food wherever you can find an empty spot?

If you use the latter method, you probably see more food spoilage. In fact, you may have to occasionally go hunting through the fridge playing an enjoyable game of "what is that smell?"

Keeping your refrigerator decluttered is a fairly easy process once you develop a system. The main goal is to keep your food easily accessible and highlight the foods that need to be eaten soonest.

Before we get started, you first have to **clear out all the expired food**, and this includes all those jars in the door you've had for 5+ years. Yes, mustard CAN expire.

Now that you have only edible food in your refrigerator, **think about how you want to use it**.

Dedicate space for frequent meal preparation: We had yogurt with granola virtually every day for breakfast along with a fruit/vegetable smoothie. One shelf of our refrigerator had yogurt and the refrigerated shake ingredients so we could easily grab them first thing in the morning.

Showcase the foods that will spoil soon by having them front and center. This will encourage you to use them in meal preparation. Our friend Angela makes it fun by adding an "Eat Me!" label to the shelf. Clear containers also make it easy to see what's inside.

Control the environment: Check the temperature to make sure foods are properly stored. Our refrigerator consistently stayed too cold, so we had to keep the setting quite low. We also put liners in the vegetable and fruit bins to help absorb any moisture that could make our fruits and vegetables too cold and hasten the spoilage.

Develop a rotation system: When you buy new food, make sure you put it behind your older food. This keeps your food waste low and your budget on track.

Don't forget the freezer: If it is older than 6 months, it is probably freezer burned by now and can be tossed. Store your foods in airtight containers or bags and push out all the excess air before you label them (include the date). No more freezer-burned "mystery meat" for dinner, and no more wasted food.

To keep your refrigerator decluttered, **go through it once a week** to identify foods that need to be eaten soon and toss what is no longer edible. To find out how long you can refrigerate or freeze foods, you can print out this food guide from the FDA to hang on your refrigerator:

www.fda.gov/downloads/Food/ResourcesForYou/Health Educators/ucm109315.pdf

Once your refrigerator is decluttered, you'll save money by having less food spoilage and eat better because all of your food is easy to find.

Kitchen Recap

How do you feel about your kitchen now? We've made some good progress this week with only a minimal amount of time spent decluttering. It doesn't take long to make an impact.

We've decluttered our tables and countertops so we can enjoy a bigger workspace and time with our families.

Then we evaluated our stock of dishes and utensils and made a plan to downsize to only what we really use.

The pantry was next, and we threw out all expired food and sorted based on need, not size.

Last, we organized the refrigerator and freezer to prevent food spoilage.

Each of these tasks should only take 1-2 hours to complete. Remember, we are not cleaning and organizing so much as decluttering and setting up systems to prevent the clutter from coming back. Don't over-think it; just do it.

Weekend Challenge

This weekend, take some time to enjoy your new space.

- Buy some good food for your body and store it in your newly organized pantry and refrigerator.

- Have dinner at the dining room table and enjoy preparing it on your clutter-free counters.

- Recycle your paper, plastic, cans and glass from the week.

- Donate your excess dishes to someone less fortunate so they can enjoy a beautiful meal like you do.

Chapter 5: Home Office

Do you work from home, even occasionally? We all know what a great experience this can be, giving you some extra free time in your day without a commute and the flexibility to start dinner while you work or run a few personal errands on your lunch break close to home.

But when your home invades the office or your work spills out into your personal space, there can be a problem. Work is no longer productive, and home is no longer the sanctuary from the outside world it used to be.

Decluttering your home office area will help you work more efficiently and retain a space for relaxation and fun with your family and friends.

In designing a lifestyle, you have to consciously think about how you want to live and take the appropriate steps to make it happen. If having a great space for thinking, writing, surfing, and working is part of your dream lifestyle, you have to decide how it will fit into your lifestyle. Take some time today to evaluate each of these scenarios in your own life and how you will manage them going forward.

If you don't feel energetic and creative in your home office, it is time to make some changes.

Taming the Paper Tiger

Before we start decluttering the office, we have to address one big issue: Paper.

If you don't solve this issue now, decluttering will only provide temporary relief. It is like going on a diet and then resuming your old eating habits as soon as the weight is gone. And we all know what happens after that.

So let's think about your paper situation for a minute.

- **Mail**: Do you have a system for sorting and acting upon your mail, or do you let it stack up?

- **Printer**: Is it always necessary to print what you've been printing? Are you just doing this out of habit or a belief you need to keep physical copies?

- **Magazines/newspapers**: Are you keeping stacks of them for articles you want to save or because you haven't gotten around to reading them yet?

- **Books**: Do you have a lot of "extra" books on the shelf? You know the kind: airplane reading, vacation books, and the latest thriller.

- **Educational material**: You went to a great seminar and brought home the 3-ring binder and associated materials intending to keep up with it. But you haven't, and now it is taking up space.

If you don't make it a practice to take out at least as much paper as you bring in, you will soon be drowning in paper. Maybe you already are.

A system for dealing with incoming paper products is the only way to keep your home office in balance. When your office is free of clutter, you can do your best work, whether that is paying bills, writing the great American novel, or even just relaxing while surfing the Internet.

Mail

We all get mail, and most of it junk. Here are some suggestions for managing your mail load as well as acting upon it right away.

- **Catalogs** encourage you to spend money, and if you are also budgeting to reach a goal this is a bad scenario. Catalog Choice gives you the power to remove yourself from all your unwanted catalog subscription lists (www.catalogchoice.org).

- **Magazines** are enjoyable, but if you are getting more than you can read it is time to cut some of them out. Let your unwanted subscriptions run out, and set up a system for recycling your magazines after 2 weeks. Cut out any articles/recipes you want to save and file them or, better yet, scan them into your computer for reference. Evernote is an excellent way to store all your scanned articles, plus it includes text recognition which makes searching for an article so much easier. We keep all our recipes and saved articles here. Evernote is free and available at www.Evernote.com.

- **Bills**: Start receiving and paying your bills online in order to prevent the paper from ever entering your home. Most banks offer this service for free and most companies encourage you to get electronic bills because it saves them money, too. You can set up payment dates as soon as you get your bill so it is instantly taken care of and will be paid on the due date without any further action from you.

Printer

How often do you use your printer and why? Do you print out driving directions from Google, articles you want to read, or receipts from online purchases? How about your schedule or important emails? (Evernote is also a good use for articles, directions and receipts since it has a notebook system and syncs to your mobile devices.)

All of these things have their uses, but what happens when you arrive at your destination, you read the article, and you have an email confirmation of your purchase? Or your day of appointments is finished and important emails dealt with?

Having a system for recycling this paper is important, or you will always have papers in your car, on your desk, or around the house. When a paper is no longer useful to you, it should be shredded or recycled. Be ruthless, especially when you have a backup online or you can easily retrieve the information elsewhere.

Some online options for items you would otherwise print:

Email labels/folders can be helpful in locating important emails. We both use Gmail and find the search feature is excellent for tracking down any emails we need.

Use a system like HighRise (highrisehq.com) to manage contact information and get rid of all those business cards and address books. You can even copy emails to this service and have them automatically filed in the proper online folder. We've been using this inexpensive service for 2 years now and love it.

Once you arrive at your destination with your Google map or otherwise finish with a piece of paper, make it a practice to fold it a certain way. Once you see a paper folded like that, you know it is safe to recycle or use as notepaper. This prevents you from having to evaluate each piece of paper you find before discarding it, wasting valuable time.

Magazines and newspapers

Do you have time to read a daily newspaper as well as multiple magazines per week? If not, you should nip this problem in the bud rather than find a way to manage it.

Cancel subscriptions to magazines you don't read right away or let them run out.

Evaluate whether a daily newspaper is right for you. Sunday delivery plus visiting the website daily during the week might be all you need.

Subscribe to neighborhood blogs. Many cities and neighborhoods have dedicated blogs. You can find out what's going on in the neighborhood by subscribing to the blog via newsletter.

Books

If you are a serious scholar or collect books of a certain type you will likely need to make room for them in your life. But for most people, books seem to pile up and we have no intention of reading them again. Paperbacks from the beach, quick reads from the airport, or even the latest bestseller – these are all fun, quick reads that should be passed on to someone else rather than shelved at your house.

Almost every town has a used bookstore, and if you start buying books there as well you can partially subsidize your reading habit and save money. You'd be surprised at how many new titles are available at used bookstores. You typically get a higher trade amount for store credit than you do for cash.

You can also set up a program to trade books with friends, or you can sign up for any of the online services that promote book sharing, like PaperbackSwap (www.paperbackswap.com).

Following our decluttering rules you can set up a system that for every new book that comes in an old book has to go.

Educational material

Whether you went for work or for self-improvement, you have probably taken some type of course as an adult that generated at least one 3-ring binder of information and possibly some books and CDs to go along with it. All attractively packaged, of course.

Most of us take these home, stick them on the bookshelf and never look at them again. Is this the situation at your house? If so, just take out the papers and recycle them now. Then use the 3-ring binder for something else or donate it to the nearest school.

If you plan to use the material, consider how it will best work for you. Perhaps you can keep one big binder and set up sections to house your most important seminar material from the last 5 years and throw the rest away. You can even stick DVDs in a plastic 3-ring holder that fits in the binder and recycle the cases. Even better, scan all the documents and store it all in your new Evernote file. You will save the space and have an easier way to access the information from anywhere.

There is no way you need every scrap of paper from every seminar you ever attended. One great system for keeping this under control is to decide on the last day of the seminar what is important and what is not and get rid of it on the spot and donate the binder back to the teacher. You'll have an easier time getting it home, especially if you are flying.

Electronics

Remember when we all had a single-line phone at home and a home office often didn't contain a computer?

Most people now have at least one cell phone and computer in the house, not to mention all the other gadgets that keep us connected and entertained.

How do you keep your portable electronics uncluttered? More importantly, how do you keep the cords straight?

Gadget organizers

Many people opt for a charging station to keep all portable electronics in one place. A Charger Station is one option for keeping everything neat and in one place. We bought one for Betsy's dad last year for Father's Day and he loves it. (Google "charger station" or "gadget organizer" to find one to fit your needs.)

Corral your cords

If you don't want to use a gadget organizer (in the end it is just another thing you own), consider labeling and organizing your cords. This will make your space neater and lessen the chance that you unplug the wrong thing. You'll also prevent wondering what cord goes with what gadget, or having a box of unknown cords in the closet that you keep for some unknown reason.

There are plenty of options for cord organizers, from the very low-cost masking tape to the still pretty cheap cord organizers from 3M. We like these because they can hold the cords to the wall, and if you have pets you know why this is important. Our dog unplugged Warren's keyboard many times while "burying" bones and taking naps under the desk. (Google "3M cord organizer" to find them online or at a nearby office supply store.)

Surge protectors

A surge protector (or two) is a wise investment. Not only does it protect your gadgets from surges of electricity due to storms and power outages, it also keeps your plugs neatly aligned. If your cords are labeled, this makes crawling under your desk to troubleshoot a whole lot easier.

Donating old electronics

Once you start organizing your gadgets, you may run across a few that you don't need anymore. Anything with dust is a good candidate, as are duplicate products.

In our home office, Warren found an old cell phone and charger. Also he found the camera we had dropped in the sand. We finally had to admit was not going to work again, no matter how hard we wanted it to.

Resources to recycle/donate/dispose of your old electronics:

- Earth911 will help you find recycling centers for all of your electronics in your zip code. We were surprised to find out how many are available. (earth911.com)

- Donate your old cell phones to battered women's shelters. They are still configured to dial 911 even without a cell phone plan. Be sure to include the charger.

- You can sell/give away boxes of cords on Craigslist or at garage sales. Believe me, we've done it. Your junk is going to be someone else's treasure.

Computer Clutter Cleanup

Everyone's computer or laptop looks about the same on the outside. After you turn it on, however, all that changes.

Quick computer clutter quiz (say that 3 times fast!):

- How many emails are in your inbox?

- Do you have folders, or do you dump everything in My Documents?

- Do you have a system for naming files so you can easily find them?

- Do you have a backup system and use it regularly?

- Do you have a temporary folder for downloads you don't need to keep?

Having a decluttered computer means you will likely work more effectively, play more creatively, and manage your personal files more efficiently.

Managing email effectively

If you have hundreds or thousands of emails in your inbox, you will soon reach a maximum and be prevented from receiving or sending. Do you really need all those emails? The easiest plan we found was switching to Gmail (mail.google.com). There is a simple search field that allows you to find any email you want, and the conversations are threaded so you can view the entire history. No muss, no fuss. Just remember to archive your emails instead of deleting them. Star or add important emails to your to-do list, and you're done. It's just that easy.

Simplifying files and folders

Setting up a system for naming your files and folders will save you hours of time in the future. Don't believe us? Betsy is a reformed "file dumper" who has used this system for the last 4+ years with great success. *"I came kicking and screaming to this format and now would never go back."*

- Make a few specific folders for your current work and separate specific folders for archive. An example would be "Bathroom Remodel_Current" and "Bathroom Remodel_Archive." Your current documents will be easy to access, and when you are done with those projects they will be stored completed in an archive file. Current documents should be easy to access – you can even put them on your desktop. Archive folders are not accessed often and can be filed away more deeply.

- When you move a project from current files to archive, be sure to only save the final versions or essential documents. All the earlier drafts and temp files should be deleted. Because you've stored everything in a "current" folder, you can simply delete it once you move the final versions to the "archive" folder.

- Use a naming convention that helps you locate documents. For pictures you may use Date_Person_Location (2009_Mom_Maui), or for client files LastName_FirstName_Project (Jones_Jack_WebsiteCopy). Your naming convention should make sense to you both now and a year from now.

- Set up a junk file for temporary downloads and files you know you don't need to keep. You can easily delete this once a week or once a month.

- The goal is to keep your computer clutter-free and well organized so you can do your best work.

- Rather than do a complete decluttering of your files (which can be mind-numbing and take a whole day or more), we recommend decluttering your current files, setting up the file system and naming convention you want to use, and just start fresh. As you access old files, you can rename them.

Spend an hour a week working on the clutter, but don't let it get in the way of starting fresh with a new system. You'll eventually get there and have great habits formed in the meantime.

Backup Systems

Even if your computer is "just for home" and you don't use it for work, think about all those pictures. If your computer crashes without a backup, you will lose them all. Don't procrastinate about getting a backup. You can get an external hard drive and make it a regular practice to back it up every week, or you can take the smart/lazy route and opt for an automatic online backup. We actually do both since we travel full-time now and don't want to risk losing our pictures from theft or damage.

Several sites offer this backup service, and you can schedule it to run every day or every week while you are sleeping. Just remember your login information (perhaps in Evernote) should anything ever happen to your computer, and you can retrieve all your photos and documents when you replace or fix your computer.

- Carbonite is the service we use (http://pop.to/13ijd)

- Mozy is another alternative that gets good reviews (http://mozy.com/)

- iDrive says once you install and log in you can be 2 clicks from protecting your data. (http://www.idrive.com/)

Converting photographs to digital files

If you have a large amount of "old school" pictures from before the digital age, get them professionally scanned now (or do it yourself if you have the time). You will love being able to enjoy them along with your more recent pictures, and you won't be disappointed at the deterioration of the actual photographs when you know you can reprint them anytime you want.

We had all of ours scanned for pennies a picture and got a thumb drive with all the images loaded in just minutes from a rep at Heritage Cards. Betsy attended a "scanning party" where everyone brought photos, drank wine, and laughed at old pictures. Google it to find a rep in your area (we're pretty sure the hostess gets free scanning). You can also Google "picture scanning in (your town)" to find other options locally. We have also helped Betsy's mom scan her pictures with a portable scanner she bought from PanDigital (pandigital.net).

You'll kill 2 birds with one stone because you can now sort your pictures online and email them to your relatives when you can't remember the name of that guy in the green bellbottoms with the mustache. Because these things are important, you know.

Separating Work from Home

If you work from home even part-time, you know how hard it can be without the proper setup and boundaries.

Working at the kitchen table or in a corner of the bedroom or family room over any length of time will cause you to stop thinking of those spaces as "home" and more like "work." And who wants work to interfere with a great dinner, spending time with the family, or getting enough rest?

Potential health problems from a poorly designed workspace

- Back and shoulder pain from tables that are too high or chairs that are not meant for hours of sitting

- Eyestrain and headaches from working in low-light environments

- Distraction from television and family conversation prolongs your work time

- The biggest problem, though, is that you soon find yourself working all the time as a lifestyle. You repeatedly check email, carry your laptop with you wherever you go, have halfhearted conversations with your family because you are distracted by work, and you go to bed and wake up thinking about work.

Are you living the lifestyle you want, or did you fall into an all-work lifestyle through circumstance and lack of planning?

Creating boundaries

Betsy worked from home for most of the 10 years before we left, both as an employee and as her own boss. "I made just about every mistake you can think of, including making work my lifestyle. I did not actively choose that lifestyle; I just fell into it for lack of anything else going on in my life at the moment. And when something great did come along, it was really hard to change my patterns."

If you are interested in creating a bigger boundary around working at home and having a personal life, here are the things we've learned (mostly the hard way):

- **Dedicate a space in your home for work**. Don't work anywhere else, and don't do anything personal in your workspace (anymore than you would do in a cubicle at a corporate office, of course).

- **Get a good chair**. Really, don't skimp on this. A proper chair will make you want to work at your desk, save your back and neck from pain, and further identify the space as "work" and not "home."

- **Take a shower, please**. As tempting as it can be to work in your PJs all day, taking a shower and getting dressed like a regular person will motivate you to act like a regular person. When a friend calls for lunch, you can pick up and go. When your spouse comes home in the evening, you look like the attractive person s/he married and not a slob. You will simply have more energy for your life if you dress for it.

- **Set up regular working hours and stick to them**. The benefit of working from home is that you often get to set your own hours. But watching television from 10-2 or taking a nap in the middle of the day just means you'll have more work to do in the evening, which takes time away from your personal life. Enjoy the flexibility, but exercise restraint.

- **Home is home and work is work**. If possible, isolate your work area from your home area. You can do this by dedicating a separate room, adding a room divider/screen, or literally throwing in the towel*. Another option is to turn your computer off at the end of the workday so it isn't as easy to "just check email for a second." Betsy even turned off the ringer on her phone at the end of each day so she wouldn't be tempted to answer.

*A friend of ours uses a large beach blanket to cover her work area when she's done for the day.

Home Office Recap

Are you feeling less overwhelmed by your home office space? We've covered a lot of ground:

- Gaining control of the paper that comes into your home
- Clearing out old electronics and creating a permanent home for your favorite gadgets
- Simplifying your computer filing system and gaining control of email
- Creating a boundary between work and home
- In addition, you've gotten resources to recycle, donate, or sell your unwanted items

Weekend Challenge

Follow through on all your good intentions by donating, recycling or listing for sale all your unwanted home office items. It doesn't count as decluttering if those boxes and bags stay in your house or garage. Let someone else get some benefit from those items, and give yourself a few more Dollars/Euro/Baht in your pocket.

Chapter 6: Closets

This is the usually first area of a home to get cluttered. Why? Because of the door. We start out with just a few boxes in the floor, then we add some to the shelf, and before long we're hanging clothes we don't wear and shoving vacuum cleaners, shoes, electronics, holiday decorations, blankets and bags of clothes for donation in a space that is meant for maybe 1/4 of that. Then we quickly slam the door and no one's the wiser.

When you fill up the closet space in your home with things that are not meant to be stored there (or stored at all), you push the things that should be in there out into your living space. Wouldn't it feel great to reclaim this space for its original purpose and leave all the corners, areas behind the doors, and unused chair seats free of clutter? Let's do it.

We keep a lot of memories in our closets: the dress we wore when we were at that "perfect" size, the suit that made us look great at that job interview 5 years ago, those high heels that hurt our feet but we can't get rid of them because they cost so much, and especially those jeans that we are determined to get back into.

In fact, most people only wear 20% of the clothes in their closets.

If you keep focusing on what you were in the past you have no time to think about the present or the future. And your closet may be reminding you every morning of who you were instead of who you are. What kind of way is that to start the day?

The Initial Purge

The first step in a closet declutter is an initial purge. You won't get all of it on this go-round, but you should be able to make a big dent in the 80% of clothes you don't actually wear.

A few guidelines for a successful closet purge:

- You haven't worn it in the last 12 months? Donate it to someone who can use it.

- Is it completely out of style or the wrong look for you? Get rid of it.

- Are there any tears, stains or broken zippers? If you haven't fixed it by now, you probably aren't going to. Toss it.

- Do you really wear all of those shoes? Donate the ones you don't actually use.

- Belts, scarves, hats – people either wear them or they don't. If you don't, get rid of them.

By now you have a pile of clothes and shoes on your bed ready for donation or the dumpster. But we still have a few steps to go.

The Importance of Sorting

You may think this idea is a little bit obsessive, but we promise it will make your life easier. This is by far the best strategy we employed to put our closet on a major diet.

First hang your clothes by type and then by color within those types. You'll hang all your pants together, sectioned off by work, casual, and dressy. Then you'll sort your pants within those sections by color. The same goes for shirts, skirts, jackets, dresses, and suits. When you do this, getting dressed every morning will be a breeze. You can easily find the pieces you are looking for, and making new outfits becomes easier. You'll also finally discover just how many pair of black pants you own, making it a little bit easier to give some of them away.

The other bonus to this system is when doing laundry. You will find clothes easily going into their assigned "slots" with a waiting hanger. No need to cram them into the closet or search for an available hanger (as a matter of fact, you should have plenty of extra hangers now!)

Set up a Passive Purge System in Your Closet

We all have clothes we think we'll wear, or we paid a lot of money for, or we consider them "investment" pieces (even though they don't fit). This tip is going to help you sort through those items.

If you have worn an item in the last 2 weeks, you can leave the hanger as is. If you have not worn it in the last 2 weeks, turn it so the hanger hooks to the closet rod from the back.

This will make it slightly more difficult for you to remove it, but it will also alert you which clothes you are not actually wearing. Once you wear the item, turn the hanger around to the front. After 3 months or a full season the clothes that are still hanging backward are clothes you should consider donating. We cannot overstate the value of this purge system in keeping your closets up to date and useful in your everyday life.

Color-Sort Your Folded Clothes

Now we'll use the same tactic for folded clothes we used with our hanging clothes. First, sort your clothes by type and color. For those that have not been worn in the last 2 weeks, turn them backward so you can determine if you are really wearing them over time. As you wear them and return them to the shelf, turn them back toward the front. This way you can easily identify clothes not being worn for a season and flag them for donation.

It will take less time than you think to do all of this, and maintenance is easy because it is visually organized.

Take the time to do this, even if you haven't done the initial purge, and you'll be pleasantly surprised at how much easier it is to get dressed in the morning and manage your clothes.

And if you are looking for an even more creative idea for getting your closets under control, may we suggest the Reverse Birthday Party?

Host a Reverse Birthday Party (even if it isn't your birthday!)

When it comes to downsizing, you can easily get bogged down in not only what to get rid of, but how to get rid of it. You know by now that we are big fans of Craigslist, and we've made thousands of dollars by downsizing this way.

But what about the good stuff? You know, the things that are beautiful, distinctive, and loved but no longer serve a purpose in your life (especially if you've had a change of weight or lifestyle and still have great clothes and accessories from before).

Betsy's 39th birthday was a great opportunity to try something new. So she decided to get a little creative and host a reverse birthday party for herself with items from her closet.

What's a reverse birthday party?

Well, instead of guests bringing you gifts they take your stuff home with them. You can price your items, accept donations, or give them away, whichever suits your needs.

She called the party My Favorite Things for My Favorite People and showcased 39 of her treasured items in honor of her 39th birthday. If we had a bigger house there is no doubt she would have invited 39 friends, but it was a tight fit with half that number.

Each item had a tag telling the story of how she had acquired the item and the memory associated with it. Guests were then allowed to "shop" through the boutique in our living room and write their names on the back of the tags if they wanted the item. If no one else wanted the item, it was hers to keep. If more than one name was on the tag, we had a "style off" on the "runway" to Carly Simon's *You're So Vain*. Each person had to model the items in a distinctive way that would earn them the most votes from the crowd. The winner of the vote got to keep the item.

Highlights from the event: (from Betsy)

"My friend Karen secretly commandeered the music and blasted out Carly Simon's *You're so Vain* for the style-offs. The music (and probably the wine) gave my friends the motivation to get really creative...and in one case strip!"

"Sharing events from my past with my friends and letting them get to know the earlier version of me was a great bonding experience."

"Watching everyone wear their new items home in layers with the tags still on them was like attending a Minnie Pearl convention!"

"Reading – and crying – over the card they got for me and the surprise group gift of a heart rate monitor for my new running program was memorable. As my friend Nancy said, I can think of all my friends hugging my heart as I run around the world. Isn't that a great thought?"

"Eating the delicious white cake with coconut icing made by my friend Pat, aka The Mayor, was a highlight. It was a girls-only event, but he stopped by to drop off the cake and I so appreciate his effort in continuing the birthday tradition my mom started years ago."

"I had a hard time letting go of some of these things. But as the evening went on, my perspective changed completely. As I watched my favorite things go out the door, I realized what I'll miss most of all when we leave are my friends."

You may not need to get rid of everything you own like we did, but there are probably things you love that no longer serve a purpose in your life. Why not share them with your good friends?

10 tips for hosting your own reverse birthday party

1. If you haven't used it in a while or can't picture yourself using it soon, you may want to get rid of it. Remember that the item is just a visual reminder of memory, not the actual memory.

2. Take the time to write out tags for each item detailing the history. When you sell/donate things to your friends, they want to know those stories. It will also help you process the memory and realize that it doesn't go away just because the item does.

3. Set up a shopping area in your home. We used a sturdy shelving unit that allowed Betsy to display items as well as hang them on the sides.

4. Invite your friends and explain the idea in the invitation. Then make a list of a few of the items you have for sale to generate interest.

5. Plan to have finger food and drinks that won't be too messy. You don't want to serve Buffalo wings when people are going to be touching your (soon to be their) valued items.

6. Set up a start and stop time to the party. Betsy had a cocktail part from 4-7 because she knew a full out evening party might be too much to take. Consider that it might be emotionally hard for you and give yourself some breathing room. We also set up the first half for open shopping and the second half of the party for the style-offs and distribution of items.

7. If you are selling your items, you can price them on the description tags or go the donation route. Betsy set up a small box that looked like a piece of luggage and just asked people to drop their donations there and it worked just fine. In the end, we made as much or more money than if we had sold it all on eBay or through consignment shops and had a whole lot more fun. More importantly, you are sure your items are going to someone you love.

8. Take a picture of you, your friend, and the item. You'll likely find that the picture is a great replacement for the item because it gives you the old memory plus a new one.

9. Leftover items should be donated/sold immediately. Do not put them back in your closets.

10. Don't forget the thank-you notes/emails. If you have a picture of you and your friend with the item, share it with them. After all, this was a special night for them, too.

Closet Recap

Remember, the main goal of the project is to clear out the clothes that represent the old you, not the current you.

Because isn't your current 'you' the best 'you' yet?

Here are a few areas of discussion around closets:

Timelines: When you have a 'maybe' item, you can set up your own timeline. Some of us have more clothes than others, and we all live in different climates. The important thing is to be aware of the clothes you have and are actually wearing and make a decision on what stays and goes in your closet in your own timeline. And some things will pass the timeline and you still decide to keep them. That's okay. It's YOUR closet.

Memory clothes: We all have them - the dress you wore on a great date, the shirt you are sure still makes you look great 10 years later, the skinny jeans you wore when you lost all that weight (before gaining it back), and maybe that letter jacket from high school. Should these really be in your everyday closet? If it really means that much to you consider taking pictures of these items (or maybe a picture of you wearing them from way back?) and taping them to the inside of the closet door. You can then either store the items or donate/sell them, but either way they are out of the way of getting dressed every morning.

What if you don't have a closet? If you live in an older home you often inherit small or nonexistent closet space along with the charm. In this case, you just apply the same rules to your armoires and dressers as you would your closet, turning items backward if you haven't worn them in a while.

Remember, most people only wear 20% of what is hanging in their closets. Betsy: "I thought I had really pared down, and when I did the backward-hanger exercise for clothes that have not been worn recently I was surprised to find how many were hanging in my closet!"

Resources to Donate or Sell Your Clothes

- Good Will/Salvation Army

- Shelters

- Churches

- Dress for Success

- Consignment shops/clothing swaps

- eBay (for special or designer clothing)

Weekend Challenge

Guess what? You just earned yourself an extra few minutes every single morning for the rest of your life in getting ready for the day. You also just saved yourself time and aggravation on laundry day by making it super easy to hang your clothes in the right spots. Congratulations!

This weekend, take a picture of your decluttered closet and tape it to the inside of your closet door. This is the way it should always look, and by having a picture close by you will see when it starts getting out of hand again (not that you'll let that happen, right?).

Make sure all your donation clothes are bagged and taken to Goodwill and consignment clothes are taken to the right shops. Closets are the easiest to backslide on after a big declutter when you don't actually remove all the clutter you've just cleared. Make sure your project is complete before you call this job done.

If you plan to host a Reverse Birthday Party, use this weekend to write out the tag descriptions for your clothes and accessories and set a date for your party. Build the buzz with your friends by emailing them a list of some of the items and how many great things you're going to put up for sale.

Last but not least, remove all the extra hangers in your closet. You should only have enough to cover the number of clothes you currently own. When you can't find an available hanger, it's a warning sign you're bringing new clothes in without removing the clothes you no longer use.

Chapter 7: Bathrooms

The bathroom is where we rush to get ready in the mornings and the room we probably spend the least amount of time, yet it accumulates an awful lot of stuff: shampoo bottles, medicines, grooming products, cleaning supplies, towels, and appliances like hair dryers and electric razors. Most bathrooms even contain a mini library!

That's a lot of stuff for one small room.

If you are starting to feel a little crowded in your bathroom, it is time to declutter.

Imagine how relaxing and energizing it would be to get ready in a clean, decluttered space each morning. Imagine how easy it would be to clean such a space without all those bottles and containers rolling around, gathering dust and loose hair. It's really disgusting when you think about it, and hardly the recipe for a positive start to your day.

Safety First

Even if you think you've got it all contained in your drawers and closets, it's a health risk to keep medications, makeup, and products past their expiration dates. If you do nothing else in your bathroom, at least get rid of the old stuff.

Have you checked your expiration labels lately? Even products that do not come with a label have an expiration date. Consult the following list for items without an expiration date and then write your throw-away date on the item yourself to prevent using stale products on your body.

Shelf life of makeup

- Mascara: 4 months
- Sponges: Wash weekly and dispose of monthly
- Nail Polish: 12 months
- Lipstick: 1-4 years, throw out if it smells rancid
- Lip liner and eyeliner: 3 years
- Cleansers: 1 year
- Eye shadow: 3 years
- Foundation: 12-18 months (oil-based lasts longer than water-based)
- Blush: 2 years
- Moisturizers: 1 year

- Lotions: 1 year

Do you use disposable razors? A woman on Oprah once stated that she used hers for YEARS at a time because she was so cheap. The maximum number of times these are designed for use is 6.

Shelf life of medicines

This is where it gets scary. Keeping medicines past their expiration date means the chemicals start breaking down. The least that may happen to you is that the medicine won't work, but do you really want to take that chance? All over-the-counter medicines have an expiration date, and if you have expired prescription drugs they should be thrown out immediately. Many pharmacies participate in medication take back programs to safely dispose of expired medication. In the US, you can find one near you at www.disposemymeds.org.

Note: Do not flush medicines unless the label states it is safe to do so because this could contaminate the water. Follow the White House guidelines on prescription drug disposal by finding a drug take-back center or mixing the drugs with an undesirable substance, like coffee grounds or cat litter, and then throwing them away.

Identifying What Gets Used

Now that you have all the expired products out of your bathroom, what is left?

Let's start with the products you use every single day. This includes your shampoo, cleansers, makeup, hair products, lotions, and even razors, blow dryers and flat irons. Put them in a box and take them out of the room.

Looking at the rest, which ones do you actually use on a regular basis?

Did you buy some blue eye shadow on a whim and know you'll never use it?

How about that soap you were given as a gift that smells too flowery to actually use?

Have a ton of hotel mini bottles of shampoo and lotion? These are welcomed at battered women shelters.

You can easily gather your loose items into groupings: a basket for spa products when you feel the need to be pampered, a basket for nail polish and manicure supplies, or a basket for special makeup for nights out - glittery products, wilder colors, etc.

When you sort your items this way, it makes the everyday use of your bathroom much easier. Storage of these non-daily items should be in harder-to-reach places, leaving your daily items front and center. Bring back your dailies and put them in convenient places for your morning grooming ritual.

What's left? Well, the stuff that probably needs to be disposed of or recycled. Don't think about the money you spent or the intentions you had to bring frosty pink lipstick back into style.

Just let it go. You'll thank yourself tomorrow morning.

Linens

Most people don't think about this one, but linens can take up an awful lot of space. We know single people who have upwards of 30 towels. How could you ever use so many?

The biggest problem with having way too many linens is how they pile up your life, letting you drag out your laundry days because of your huge supply. Before long, you have 2 or 3 loads of towels waiting to be washed along with 2 changes of bedsheets. Your linen closet is full of clean towels and your hamper or floor is full of dirty ones. Your life is more complicated and messy because you simply have too many options.

(This is just like having all those plastic drinking cups in your kitchen.)

When you narrow your selection down to what you need every week plus one replacement set for laundry day, you declutter your space and simplify your options. Of course it takes a regular washing schedule to keep this plan on track, but you should be doing that anyway.

Consider how often you launder, how many days you use your towels, and come up with a reasonable number to keep. A good indicator you have too many towels or sheets is that you never get to the bottom of the stack. The same goes for your sheets. You probably have a favorite pair anyway. Why keep the ones that always come undone from the mattress or feel stiff on your skin? Donate these barely-used linens to Good Will or to your friends who may be just starting out or starting over (such as college or divorce).

Cleaning Supplies

Whether you keep your cleaning supplies in the bathroom or not, now is when we declutter them. The first step is to go around your house and gather all your cleaning supplies in one place, like your kitchen table. (If you have too many cleaners to fit on your kitchen table, we have our work cut out for us!) Check your closets, under your sinks, in the pantry, the linen closet, and on the floor of your bathrooms.

Group your supplies by job, like all floor cleaning products together, all dusting supplies together, all bathroom cleaning supplies, etc.

Now that you can look at them, are you surprised at how many you have? When your home is cluttered, you often can't find what you're looking for, so you assume you don't have it. You make a trip to the store and buy another bottle, brush, or gadget, further cluttering your home and depleting your budget.

Now you are going to consolidate your cleaning supplies and make it easy for you to find them every time you need to clean. You'll also know exactly what kind of supplies you have at all times so you avoid over buying in the future.

First, let's combine like bottles together where possible. If you have 2 half-full bottles of Mr. Clean, combine them together and recycle the empty bottles. (Warning: Do not combine partial cleaning products unless they are identical products. You can make yourself very sick by mixing chemicals.) Not everything will be able to be combined, like multiple Comet canisters, but do the best you can. Over time you're going to use up your duplicates so it won't be a problem for long.

Your collection should be smaller by now, but it is still probably too large. Don't worry; we're going to fix this problem. First, think about how you clean your home and what system of storing your cleaning supplies would work best for you. If you live in a small apartment, grouping your cleaning supplies in one box is probably sufficient. You can simply carry it with you as you clean. We find this method perfect because we live in small spaces and do our cleaning all at once.

If you have a larger home, multiple stories, or clean your house in stages on different days, you may want to keep a box of supplies on each floor or a small box of appropriate supplies in the kitchen and each bathroom or hall closet. This decision is up to you, but the goal is to keep just enough of what you need in a form convenient for you to use. More is not necessarily better, and when you have supplies scattered all over the house, it will be harder to keep track of them and find them when you need them.

When you package your boxes of cleaning supplies in whatever format you deem best for you, don't forget to include cloths, brushes, and all the tools you need to clean. Use your half-full bottles of products and put all your extras – your stash of full backup supplies – in your garage or a shelf in your closet. This is where you will go to replenish your supplies when your boxes get low. At all times your active cleaning supplies are in your boxes and your backups are waiting in the replenish area. You shouldn't need to buy more than 1 backup item at a time so your replenish station is small and easy to store.

The goal is to make your cleaning chores easier by consolidating your tools in a way that makes sense to you and your home. We can't promise you'll actually like cleaning after you declutter your cleaners, sponges, brushes, trash bags, cloths, mops, brooms, and dust pans, but at least you'll have more space in your home and more money in your bank account after you stop overstocking.

Bathroom Recap

The week is over and you now have a junk-free bathroom in which to get ready for your day and relax and unwind with a bath in the evenings. Like your bedroom closet, having a clutter-free zone for getting ready in the morning means you'll start your day calm, energized, and on time.

We've addressed the main areas of clutter accumulation in a bathroom: grooming products, medications, linens and cleaning supplies. If you follow one of the 5 decluttering strategies we outlined at the beginning of the book, you'll be able to keep your bathroom in check. Bringing in a new tube of lipstick means getting rid of the old one. A broken shaver or blow dryer should be recycled or tossed. If you get new towels for Christmas, donate the same number of old towels.

Remember, the point is not to keep accumulating, but to keep your possessions at the optimum number for efficiency and space – especially in the smallest room of your house.

Weekend Challenge

Now that your bathrooms have been streamlined, it's time to take away the excess. Expired medications should be taken to your local medication take-back center or disposed of via cat litter or coffee grounds in your trash. Empty containers should be recycled and junk should be taken to the trash. Your new box of cleaning supplies should be stored in a designated spot, and your backup supplies should be together in a different place. Excess towels and sheets should be taken to your local Goodwill or given to a friend who really needs them.

It's easy to think because this room is so small you can breeze through the cleanup, but it is precisely because it is so small it gets cluttered fast. Be sure to finish out your chores on this room or you'll see it back in a disaster state by next week.

Reward yourself for the week's work by lighting a candle and giving yourself a nice long soak in the tub as you admire your handiwork. Remember, less stuff to maintain means more time to spend on you, and that's pretty nice at the end of a long week.

Chapter 8: Garage/Attic/Storage Building

Your living space also includes the space outside your primary living area. We're talking about your garage, attic, carport, or storage building. This is where we put things we don't know what else to do with, everything from vehicles to sports equipment to books to half-finished projects and even trash. You may also store your memories out here, though you'll have to refer to Chapter 3 to remind yourself that if it is a treasure, it should be treasured.

If you have a problem with clutter in your home and own any of these type of storage spaces, you are likely facing your biggest challenge here. It is so easy to put things in a space you don't see every day, or at least one you can close the door on and hide from company. It's secret junk, for the most part, and like any secret it gets bigger over time.

Today we're going to shed some light on your secret and get it organized so you can start using this space instead of hiding things in it.

Are you parking your car in the garage? If you are still scraping the ice from your windshield every winter morning before work because you have too much junk in the garage to fit your car, then you are making life unnecessarily difficult for yourself. If the summer sun bakes the interior of your car and takes your breath away (along with a layer of skin) when you sit down, then you are making your life unpleasant when you don't have to.

The garage is meant to be a place to store your car or perform small household or automotive repair jobs. You might even want to take up a hobby in here. It is not meant to hold all the boxes from your last move five years ago that wouldn't fit inside your new home. If you haven't used them in five years, do you really think you ever will?

We have a friend who moved cross-country 3 times with the same 40 boxes of books over the course of 15 years. Imagine the weight, space, and money it took to maintain this collection of industry books she thought she couldn't live without! When she finally came to her senses, she spent one day going through them all and discovering they were too outdated to even donate to her local business group. She ended up recycling almost every single one.

This is the price you pay when you indiscriminately store boxes in your garage for years or decades at a time. Things break down due to extreme temperatures, become outdated, get crushed, suffer water damage, and get dirty or nibbled on by mice. You lose the use of your garage, attic, or storage building for practical storage, like sports equipment, out-of-season clothes, or even your car and bicycles.

We once helped some friends clean out their garage. No, we didn't do this for fun, though we have to admit we had some. These friends had just consolidated a big chunk of their business into their personal garage, and they needed help getting their space back.

Enter the Craigslist Guru, also known as Warren. Our garage had been clean for years by the time we were called to help, so it was a great refresher on how to organize an out-of-control garage.

Here is a very effective method you can use repeatedly over several weekends to almost effortlessly clean out your garage. Reread Chapter 2 a few days before so you've got your Craigslist selling plan in place.

- Assemble a team of at least 3 people: your mate, your kids, the neighbors (if you promise to help them later), friends, or relatives

- Assign one person as the picture taker/ad poster; everyone else sorts/moves/cleans

- Pull out the first 3-5 things you want to sell, preferably the big items.

- Clean them off, take pictures, and post the ads on Craigslist.

- Continue the above process along with checking email for ad responses every 15 minutes.

- Encourage potential buyers to purchase that day by offering a slight discount or bonus item. Let them know you're doing an extreme garage cleanout today.

- Take only cash (state it in the ads).

- Keep in touch with interested buyers until the item is sold. The first person that says he wants it doesn't always show up, so you can go back to #2 and #3 if necessary.

That's it. Using this strategy, you can clean out a good portion of your garage in one afternoon because people are moving/sorting/cleaning while ads are going out and people are coming to buy.

People will continue contacting you about the remaining items over the next several days. Getting this done on a Friday will encourage sales through the weekend, and by Monday you'll be looking at a far less cluttered garage.

We can't promise that your garage cleaning experience will be fun (though it might be with good friends and a pizza), but with a system it can be fairly quick and mostly painless (especially when you start counting the cash!).

Garage/Attic/Storage Building Recap

Once you've streamlined your main storage space, you'll find it a more active part of your life. You might be able to store your car every night or actively use your space to store out-of-season clothes and equipment. This will be a rotating space used by you to make your life inside your home more efficient, relaxing, and stress-free.

Like the other rooms, you'll use one of the 5 decluttering strategies you learned in Chapter 1 to keep it organized when you are done. The effort you make over the course of a few weekends can be easily maintained for years to come with regular attention to the decluttering strategy you pick. It is 100% mental, and thinking about it before you bring home something new or casually toss something out in the garage will prevent you from having to bribe your friends (and yourself) to give up a few weekends to clean it out.

Your garage and attic are for storage of things you actually use throughout the year. When you fill it with crap you don't use, you defeat the purpose of having a garage or storage building.

Weekend Challenge

Your weekend is going to be challenging enough in getting this done, so here are some tips to help you prepare and recover.

Appreciate what your friends are helping you do. This is hard work, and many hands make it easier. Keep your friends interested by not dragging down the process. No one wants to have to talk you into selling something you obviously don't need anymore, and if you make it hard for your friends to clean, move, photograph, and place the ads – not to mention closing the deal with interested buyers – they won't stick around long. It's the weekend, and they have better things to do than watch you defend your junk. Remember, they are doing you a favor, so don't make it hard for them. And don't forget to feed them!

When the work is done, move the remaining items back, but make sure you can easily get to them. Throughout the week you may have buyers contacting you, and you'll want an easy way to display and remove the item if a buyer comes over.

Don't think about what you paid for the item when pricing. Just like you wouldn't pay big bucks for a customized couch for someone else's decor, neither will someone else do this for you. The price you paid for an item has absolutely nothing to do with the price you will sell it. The only thing that matters is the current market for the item and your level of motivation to get rid of it. If you don't know what an item should cost, do a quick Google or Craigslist search to find out how similar used items are priced.

As you finish out your day, be sure to recycle your boxes and take out the trash from the day's effort. Leave the garage as uncluttered as possible so you'll be incented to continue the process the next weekend. It won't be long until you're using this space instead of just filling it up!

Chapter 9: Final Notes on Decluttering

If you've been working in conjunction with this book, you have already accomplished a lot, from learning the basic decluttering styles all the way down to disposing of your old medicine. Doesn't it feel great to know how much more room you have than when you started this book?

Whether you made a huge impact on your space or simply needed to straighten up a drawer or two, give yourself a pat on the back. You absolutely deserve it. You have taken the first steps towards a life with less clutter. Learning to let go of the junk serves two purposes:

1. It frees your space, both figuratively and literally, so you can create the life you want.

2. It teaches you that you don't have to keep everything in life that comes to you. What you allow to stay in your life is a choice, *your choice*. And yes, again we're speaking both figuratively and literally.

If you haven't get gotten started, you now have the guideline to develop your strategy. While it is important to plan, ***it is more important to act***, and we encourage you to get started in even a small way right away. Time is the enemy here, and if you don't do something soon you'll put this book away and the sense of urgency will fade.

It is important to remember that the process is ongoing. Even if you completely declutter your home today, tomorrow will present a new challenge in keeping it that way. You can spend a lot of time thinking about why you are a packrat and how you let it get that way, but we prefer the action-oriented approach of knowing how you can best keep yourself on track using one of the five decluttering strategies.

Remember, thinking about your problem for so long is part of the reason it got out of hand in the first place. Replace thinking with action - a little bit every single day - and you'll keep your space and life open to the joy of living.

You may experience a few side benefits to decluttering beyond the obvious. This new lightness in your life translates to other areas, and people will notice. Whether you actually do or not, you'll feel like you've lost 10 pounds when you shed some of weight tying you down in your home. (Some people actually do experience a noticeable weight loss after decluttering!)

With a newly decluttered home, you'll start and end your day more relaxed and energized than ever before. You'll also be confident about having guests in your space, which means your social life should pick up.

Most of all, though, you'll have a greater confidence in your ability to design and create the life you want. You envisioned a better space in which to live, and you made it happen. This is a skill you can duplicate in other parts of your life. We did it, and you can, too.

Chapter 10: Life After Decluttering

We're writing this book a few years after completing our own decluttering project and selling or giving away everything we owned. This time has been a huge transformation for us both. We've been all over the world with only 12 kg (26 lbs) of possessions each. It is hard to believe we used to have enough stuff to fill a 3,000 sq ft home.

> To find out how we parlayed our initial $8000 from Craigslist sales into a 5-year travel budget, check out our book, *Dream Save Do: An Action Plan for Dreamers*, now available at www.dreamsavedo.com.

Betsy no longer views herself as a packrat. She loves the freedom that comes from being able to pick up at any moment to move in a new direction.

Warren has found that a life without plans is more exciting than he ever thought possible. By not needing to manage each day's activities, or even knowing what city we will visit next, he is more relaxed than at any point in his life.

We do not miss our things. There is not a single item we got rid of that could come close to the memories and experiences we make each and every day. The decision to give up all our possessions is the best one we ever made and we are excited to see where life will take us in the future.

You may find this hard to believe, but we don't have any physical souvenirs from our travels. But we do have a treasure trove of memories, pictures (digital of course), friendships, and experiences that will never dull or age over time.

We wish the exact same thing for you in your newly decluttered life, no matter where life's journey takes you.

Now get out there and enjoy it.

Turn the page to read an excerpt from our book Dream Save Do: An Action Plan for Dreamers.

Dream Save Do

An Action Plan for Dreamers

By Warren & Betsy Talbot

Author's Note

Hey there, you sexy dreamer. Yes, you! It's great to see you here, ready to create the life you really want.

We're writing this introduction to you from the gorgeous French Alps after a year of traveling in South America, Antarctica, and Europe, and we have the funds for four more years of travel. Yes, you heard that right. We used this exact method to amass enough cash to travel the world for five years. We know what we're talking about, and we want to help you learn to fund your dream, too.

Maybe you're planning on traveling the world, or creating something incredible like a novel or an invention, or even going back to school to be what you always wanted to be before you got sidetracked. There are as many dreams as there are people, but there are only so many ways to amass cash.

Frankly, most of them are boring or painful and therefore unlikely to work for you.

This guide will not be a run-of-the-mill plan for saving 10% of your earnings for a rainy day. Your upcoming accumulation of cash has a purpose, a mission, a real job to do, for heaven's sake. Instead, this guide is the *rain-maker* strategy for gathering the momentum and steam you need to reach your dream in the shortest possible time frame.

And, we have to admit it's more than a little bit fun.

You see, we used this exact same plan, cobbled together from our own experience chasing a dream of traveling around the world, and felt like we were already living our dream two years before it happened. Just taking action on a small part of your dream, like raising the money to do it, will give you a huge mental boost for all the other things you need to do to make your dream a reality. The minute you deposit your first bit of dream money you'll see exactly what we're talking about.

We're so excited for you we can hardly keep ourselves together!

Your dream is right around the corner, and you just took the first step toward it.

Let's get started!

Introduction

"You're so lucky!"
"I wish I could do that!"
"Must be nice!"

These are the phrases we often hear when we tell people we are traveling around the world, and they are all true. We do consider ourselves lucky to live this life, we know lots of people who wish they could do it, and yes, it is very nice.

But you know what? Luck comes from focus and action.

People want to know our secret, the magic recipe, the special power that helped us go from corporate drones to world travelers. They want to know a quick answer and we have one:

Spend less than you earn. Save what's left.

(Okay, you can throw something at us now. We deserve it.)

With dieting, you know that eating fewer calories than you use will result in weight loss. Yet many of us are overweight. With such a simple concept, we should all be thin! But you know how that goes in the real world, and it is much the same with saving money. It takes more than this basic knowledge to set yourself on a path to amassing the kind of cash that can change your life.

That is where our guide comes in. You'll get way more than a stern lecture to "spend less than you earn." You'll get step-by-step instructions on amassing serious cash with advice for challenges and pitfalls along the way.

We'll show you how to:

- Automate your savings to bypass willpower issues (hey, why test it if you don't have to?)

- Create some homemade porn to keep you motivated (but not the kind you think!)

- Build your first crappy budget and then make it into a great one.

- Combat peer pressure and possibly even make people jealous of your new thrifty lifestyle.

- Live large on a small entertainment budget.

This guide is going to show you how to stockpile loads of money in a relatively short period of time so you can create something amazing in your life. You will never, ever look at saving money as that boring old rainy day thing again.

The Big Question: How did we do it?

We know where you are right now because we've been there, too. We wanted to change our lives but we didn't know how. It wasn't until two people very close to us came down with life-threatening illnesses that we finally forced ourselves into action, and that's when we learned the biggest secret of all.

> ### *Scheming and dreaming will only fill your time. Taking action will fill your bank account.*

It doesn't matter that you don't know how something will turn out or exactly how you're going to do it. It doesn't matter that you don't know all the answers (who does, by the way?) What matters is that you take the first step, begin action immediately, and continue taking action every day until you reach your dream.

We learned this lesson as we saved and worked toward our dream, realizing that all those questions we had at the start were magically answered along the way because we were forcing them to be answered. Now you're going to learn to do the same thing.

The guide is set up in three sections:

- **DREAM:** Really define your dream and know what a day in the life looks like so you can figure out what it will actually cost.

- **SAVE:** Save, sell, find, earn: We'll show you all the ways you can amass the cash – more quickly than you thought – to finance your dream.

- **DO:** What you do is more important than what you say, and this section covers the pitfalls (and comeback strategies) as well as your new role as the Pied Piper to all your friends who watch you from the sidelines as you prepare to live your dream.

Throughout the guide you'll read specific scenarios from our story to illustrate the lessons we learned from the experience as well as how we made it through the roughest patches unscathed. Wherever you see the **Idea Generator** sections you'll find tips and questions to help you in both the creative and practical steps to the program, and you can also watch videos that we'll email to you over the coming weeks where we go into some of the steps in further detail and help you over the bumps in the road.

We'll also reveal the key components to our savings plan:

- **THE VAULT** is the account where you will keep your money. It is a one-way street. You can't touch this. In fact, imagine a big guard dog in front of your Vault door, snarling and barking if you get close (though he will wag his tail and roll on his back for a belly scratch once you reach your goal). Money goes in, but it does not come out until you have hit your goal. Do not make your guard dog bark.

- **THE ROADMAP** is your budget, the guide along this savings journey. You will start out with a crappy one, and your job is to refine it over time, making adjustments every month to move you closer to your goal. We'll show you how to do it, and we promise the only painful one will be the first one.

- **DREAM PORN** is your big visual, the reminder you place in a prominent space to keep your goal front and center.

- **PHRASE TO SAVE** is the mantra you will develop to keep you on track with your daily spending and celebrate your savings. We'll show you how to develop yours based on your budget numbers and your dream.

Finally, you'll see a checklist item at the end of each chapter to remind you of the major steps needed to complete this plan. At the end of the guide, you can download the one-page checklist of all the steps for easy reference.

Last but not least, you'll find a bonus report on how to sell your extra junk to make some cash. You don't have to go to the extreme to sell everything like we did, but we'll bet you can find a lot of stuff sitting around that isn't of use to you anymore. Let it go to work funding your dream.

We recommend that you read the guide through once, check out the bonus material, and then go back and perform the exercises and get started taking action on your dream. (Though we won't penalize you for jumping right in.)

Does that sound like a good start on learning how to live your dream? We think so. Now let's begin with putting your money where your mouth is.

Ready to get started?

Disclaimer: You know the drill. We can't guarantee you'll have the same level of success as we did, though we can't rule out you having more success than us, either. We are not financial advisers or attorneys, and we can't be held responsible for anything you do or do not do as a result of this guide.

But you already knew that.

As with most things in life, the outcome is entirely up to you.

To Read More, order your copy of *Dream Save Do* today from:

- Amazon (www.amazon.com)
- iTunes (www.itunes.com)
- Barnes & Noble (www.barnesandnoble.com)

The authors greatly appreciate you taking the time to read our work. Please consider leaving a review wherever you bought the book, or telling your friends or blog readers about *Getting Rid of It*, to help us spread the word.

We are indie authors and depend on satisfied readers to help us spread the word so we can continue to write for you.

Thank you for supporting our work.

About the Authors

Our #1 goal is to open your mind to the possibilities that exist in your life. And a very close #2 is to teach you the practical steps – actions, attitudes, and relationships – that will get you where you want to go.

You don't have to travel the world to have a fulfilling and adventurous life. But you do need to know what you really want to do and give some time and attention every to making it happen.

That's where we come in. We're Warren and Betsy Talbot, and after two serious health scares with people close to us, we decided life was too short. We asked ourselves the question, "What would we do if we didn't make it to our 40th birthdays?" For a couple of 37-year-olds, it was a pretty powerful motivator to chase our biggest dream of world travel.

We set out the very next day to make our dream a reality, and just 25 months later – after saving a lot of money and downsizing from a house to 2 backpacks – we set off on a journey of a lifetime.

We've been writing about the practical steps to creating the life your dreams in our books and on our website, www.MarriedwithLuggage.com, ever since. There you can find out more about creating the life you want from the life you already have. You'll also find our books, articles, photos, videos, and the free signup for our weekly email newsletter with life lessons from our travels. We'd love to have you join our tribe.